54 Ways

To Stay Positive
in a Changing, Challenging
And Sometimes NEGATIVE World.

Simple Choices
For More Positive Living

Written By JoAnna Brandi
Illustrated By Jo Ann Goldsmith

Published by *JoAnna Brandi & Company, Inc.*

54 Ways

To Stay Positive *in a Changing, Challenging*
And Sometimes NEGATIVE World.

Published by *JoAnna Brandi & Company, Inc.*
7491 N. Federal Hwy, C-5 #304
Boca Raton, FL 33487
561-279-0027   Fax: 561-279-9400
Email JoAnna Brandi at: joanna@customerretention.com
Visit JoAnna on the Web at: www.54simplechoices.com
& at: www.customerretention.com

Book Illustration and Cover Design by Jo Ann Goldsmith
Goldsmithing Enterprises
6216 Barton Creek Circle
Lake Worth, FL 33463
561-963-6426   Fax: 561-432-8207
Email Jo Ann at: joann@creategoldmines.com
Visit Jo Ann on the web at: www.creategoldmines.com

ISBN 978-1-930283-00-8

INTRODUCTION

"Ladies and Gentlemen, we've encountered an area of light turbulence," came the pilot's voice over the loudspeaker, the last time I flew. "We ask that you please fasten your seatbelts and remain comfortably seated."

Good advice. Wouldn't it be nice if we got such a warning every time we encountered turbulence in our lives?

Wouldn't it be nice if we could remain comfortably seated each time the winds of life tossed us around a bit? I think so. Faced with the fast-paced, fast-forward lives most of us lead, and the crazy world we live in, wouldn't it be a blessing to have some strategies for remaining calm and centered in the midst of a changing, challenging, and even sometimes negative world? Sure it would.

We all have our own ways of dealing with negativity and coping with stress. I don't know about you, but with the world being what it is, I find that I need to keep sharpening my coping skills and keep learning new ways to stay balanced in the midst of it all.

As a mother, business owner, public speaker, writer, and consultant, I have chosen a life that provides a long list of daily challenges. I've placed myself squarely in the path of challenge and change. I chose it, but goodness knows I wasn't equipped for it. So, through the years I've had to collect my own, often eclectic ways of dealing with the increasing challenges of life. Frequently in the course of my work, I share those ways with others.

A few years ago I was delivering a seminar on Customer Care. (In my business life I'm known as the 'Customer Care Lady.') During a segment on attitude, I told participants that psychologists estimate 78% of the information we take in is negative.

"How," I asked the audience, "can we stay in the 'positive, up-beat, can-do mode' most customers want if we are bombarded by negative messages?"

Rather than an answer, I was greeted with a question. A woman in the back of the room jumped up and shouted, "Tell us how JoAnna. What do YOU do to stay positive in a negative world?" I inhaled deeply and then answered. "That's a great question. I have a variety of ways. They are personal, but I would be happy to share them with you if you'd like." I continued, "If you give me time I will think about it carefully and get them back to you with my segment for your next company audiotaped newsletter. How's that?" The audience was enthusiastic at the suggestion. I was intrigued at the notion of listing some of the strategies I had collected through the years, the little things I did to help me stay centered.

That night I started listing the things I do that contribute to my ability to stay upbeat and positive in the tumultuous life I have chosen. I listed thirteen "ways." When it came time to record my segment of the company's newsletter (which, at the time, was part of my consulting contract with them) I cheerfully put forth the first 13 ways to stay positive, and promised 13 more the following month. True to my promise I delivered and happily received a positive response.

Soon I created a file folder marked "Ways to Stay Positive." I found myself adding notes to the folder and asking friends, "When you're having a tough day and start feeling negative, what do you do to pull yourself out of it?" Their responses went into the folder too. Over time the folder was stuffed with notes and ideas about simple, inexpensive, accessible ways to shift one's mood from dark to light.

Now, with all this focus on the positive, I became aware of my occasional tendencies to slip into the negative, the derogatory and the sarcastic. I started catching myself and asking "Is this the way I really choose to live my life?" "Is this a good model for what I teach?" There were times when the answer was "No." But the consciousness was what mattered. After admitting to the "No," I found I had the opportunity to change my mind and offer myself a more positive thinking choice.

More importantly, I learned to acknowledge and congratulate myself on my ability to shift my mood and make a more positive choice. For the first time, I began patting myself on the back, more, not less, than others did, and that felt great!

I have spent years attending workshops and seminars, reading books and listening to teachers who said, "You choose your state of mind." I finally began to accept that indeed, I had the power to do that. I had the power to choose a more positive way of life.

And so, I decided to turn the folder of notes into a book. I compiled 37 of my "Ways to Stay Positive" and asked a publisher friend, to tell me if he felt the book had possibilities. "Yes," he said, "I love the concept! Can you expand on it some more?" "And,' he said, "it needs pictures. It definitely needs pictures."

I thanked him and began thinking about even more of the things I did when I needed to shift myself out of a negative state. More notes found their way into the folder. One weekend, while attending a seminar, I had a breakthrough of sorts. We did a wonderful exercise on loosening up the side of your brain you don't normally use a lot. (You will find it here in this book). That night I put my pen to paper and wrote for several hours. I was able to make a list of many more strategies I use to stay positive (and hence creative.) I was surprised; there were quite a few more then I would have guessed!

When I returned home from the workshop I decided it was time to look for an artist. At every network meeting I attended and to every friend I spoke with, I asked the question "Do you know an illustrator?" Through the two years I looked, I got drawings from many, but none of them seemed to "fit" my book. Then one day, an illustrator graciously offered to work on eighteen of the "Ways" to show how he would draw them. I agreed.

The drawings came back. They were good-- catchy and cute. But not really "right." I carried them in my briefcase and pulled them out occasionally to measure my reaction. I badly wanted this artist to be the one, and almost had myself convinced it was so.

Then I visited my daughter. She's a photographer and graphic artist, and I often rely on her artistic eye. I hadn't seen her in months so I anxiously presented the drawings and waited for her reaction. (By this time I had talked myself into liking them.) I watched her face and then carefully listened as she used her best communication skills to tell me what she really thought.

"Mom," she ventured, "They are good. Really good. I agree with you that this artist is good." I began to breathe easier. "But Mom, the pictures don't really fit with your words. The meanings and feelings you want to get across get lost in these pictures. Yes, they're cute, but the book is not really about being cute, Mom. It's meaningful stuff. Don't make it happen before it's ready. Wait and be patient. You will find the right artist, or maybe the right artist will find you."

Out of the mouth of babes, but tough medicine for me to take. By this time I wanted this "project" finished (yes, it had become a "project" somewhere along the line.) I wanted a deadline!

But it seemed the demanding businessperson inside me was going to have to step aside and detach from the outcome of this project. The timing wasn't right, no matter how much I willed it to be so. So I was learning another lesson in the preparation of this work, a lesson about right timing. A few more deep breaths and I made the choice to trust that the right person would appear, at the right time. And you know what? She did.

After attending a business meeting in Fort Lauderdale, I met an artist --
Jo Ann Goldsmith. We chatted and exchanged business cards. A few months later I ran into her again, but this time I asked her more about her work.

She told me of her experience with designing catalogs and advertisements. She told me she had worked with other writers and had designed greeting cards. My next question of course was, "Are you an illustrator?" "Indeed I am, " she responded.

And the rest, as they say, is history.

Jo Ann didn't just illustrate the book. She meditated the book. Every illustration is a result of a meditation Jo Ann did after reading each concept. When you look at this book and experience her glorious illustrations, I'm sure you will feel, as I do, that perhaps they were divinely inspired. Who knows? All I know is that after years of carrying around that file folder, and years of procrastinating on delivering the final manuscript, it is time for this piece of work to be born and to be shared.

In the end, I know this book was a labor of love and, like love, it took many twists and turns in the making. But oh the lessons along the way!

I am deeply grateful to the woman at the seminar who asked an inspired question. I am deeply grateful for the Divine spark within me that kept the ideas flowing and allowed me to capture them here in a simple, easy to understand way. I am grateful to my daughter for her courage and her honesty.

And, I am very, very grateful to my collaborator, Jo Ann Goldsmith.
She gave my words life and light. She has been uncommonly patient and understanding with my slow and methodical pace. She has interacted with me in the most loving and caring ways, encouraging me to take as long as I needed, since the book would be birthed when it was ready. Most of the time she had more faith in the process than I.

At last, more than four years since it first began to take form, here it is, in its own time, ready to make its appearance. Creating this book has taught me about love and patience and integrity and timing. It is my sincerest hope that it will teach you about making simple choices, on a daily basis, that will make your life a little bit more positive, a little bit more centered, and a little bit more healthy and maybe even a little bit more whole.

So Jo Ann, we finished it! This baby is born. And she's quite beautiful, even if I do say so myself.

Let's celebrate!

DEDICATION

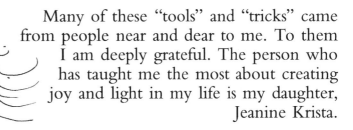

Many of these "tools" and "tricks" came from people near and dear to me. To them I am deeply grateful. The person who has taught me the most about creating joy and light in my life is my daughter, Jeanine Krista.

I dedicate this book to her with deep appreciation and gratitude for the privilege and pleasure of raising such a beautiful and bright human being.

This book is in loving memory of our dear friend Toby Litt. She lived her life fully and with great joy and touched us all with her beauty. Many blessings to her wherever she is now. She lives on in our spirits.

"Balance begins with the Breath.
Taking in and letting go are the primal rhythms of life.
Breathing in you find inspiration;
breathing out you find release."

– Dan Millman –

"Change your breath to change your life."

– Gael Chiarella –

1. BREATHE DEEPLY

Post little notes that say *breathe* all around your space. Deep breaths bring fresh oxygen into your lungs and brain.

Inhale deeply and fill your belly with air. Then fill your chest and inflate it like a balloon. Exhale and pull your tummy in. Then push the air out of your lungs.

Breathing correctly is a great abdominal exercise too. Just think of it as doing extra sit-ups. That makes me happy.

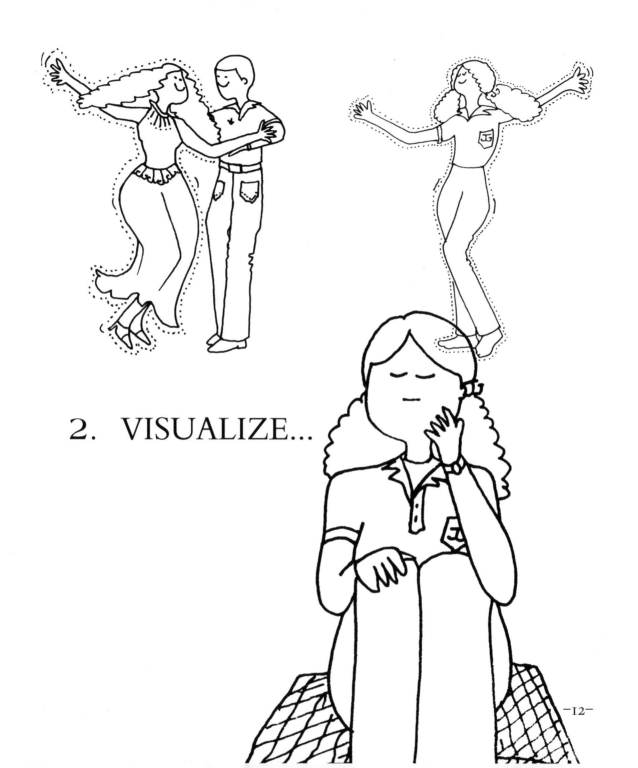

2. VISUALIZE...

Remember the mind/body connection. If you can't change what is going on in your mind, then change what is going on in your body.

First close your eyes. Now, remember a time when you felt wonderful.

With your body, recreate the experience of feeling wonderful. Guess what? Your mind will follow.

...THEN CONNECT WITH YOUR BODY

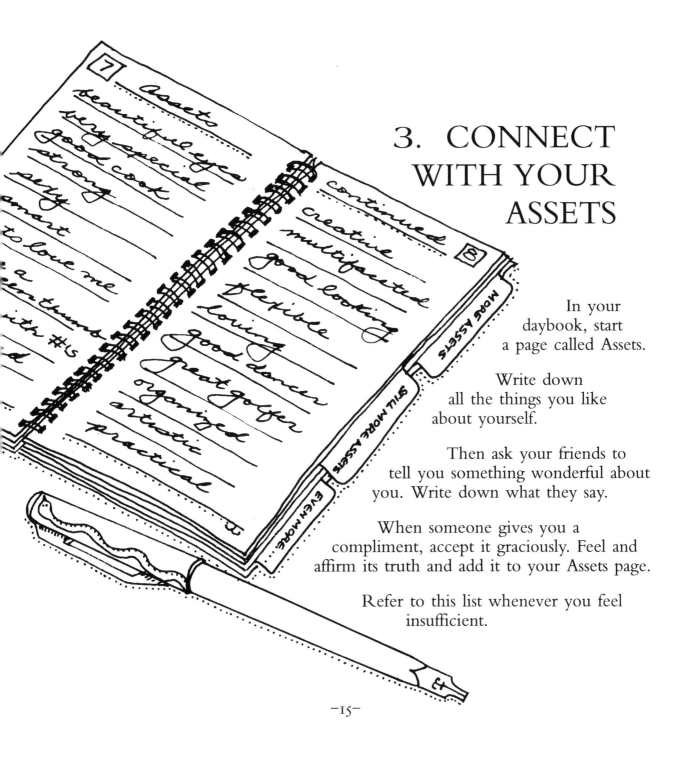

3. CONNECT WITH YOUR ASSETS

In your daybook, start a page called Assets.

Write down all the things you like about yourself.

Then ask your friends to tell you something wonderful about you. Write down what they say.

When someone gives you a compliment, accept it graciously. Feel and affirm its truth and add it to your Assets page.

Refer to this list whenever you feel insufficient.

4. LET GO OF NEGATIVE THOUGHTS

Concentrate on letting go of negative thoughts. Many of us have constant negative thoughts simply because we hold on to them.

In your mind's eye give yourself permission to let them go. Visualize your negative thoughts as clouds and let them drift easily out of sight.

P.S. You get to control the wind. Blow those negative thoughts away.

5. PROGRAM YOUR MIND

We all have the choice and the power
to *reprogram* our mental software and get different results.

A way to understand your *program* is to monitor
the things you say to yourself throughout the day.
Do you say things that nourish and grow you like *I can,
I will,* or *It's easy*? Or do you say things that hold you back
like *I can't, I shouldn't,* or *It's too hard*?

Learn to use positive affirmations and *self-talk*
to change your programs. Affirmations are positive statements
said in the present tense. They describe the state you want
to achieve.

> *I have a strong and healthy body.*
> *I find a silver lining in every cloud.*
> *Everyday I use my mind to create positive thoughts.*

I know this may sound corny, but if you do this
consistently over time, it works. Remember that the behind
follows the mind.

Move your mind. Your life will follow.

6. SAY "YES!"

Leave little notes everywhere that say *yes*.

Your office, house, and car are excellent locations for these up-beat reminders.

Add to them whenever you want to say yes.
Yes to glowing health.
Yes to love.
Yes to being smart.
Yes to creativity.

Say *yes* to whatever you want to be.

7. TURN OFF THE TV

Treat yourself to a positive outlook. Turn off the TV. Refuse to support violence and *"body bag reporting."*

Watch headline news just once a day, or read one good newspaper. Sure, you need to stay in touch, but you don't need to drown in negative media sensationalism.

Take a stand. When we stop watching the sensationalism, the media will limit its negative and violent presentations.

8. DON'T <u>SHOULD</u> ON YOURSELF!

All through our lives our parents, friends, teachers, and the media tell us what we should and should not do and be. By the time we are grown, we have accumulated a lot of shoulds.

I should do this. Go there. Do that. We have gender-related shoulds: Women should. Men should. There are job-related shoulds: *Managers should and salespeople should.* And there are even age-related shoulds. *Someone your age should.* We have *shoulds* for every role we hold.

Count the shoulds in your life. They may be weighing you down. They may be like clothes that don't fit or those you are holding on to for no reason at all. You can change some of the *I shoulds* to *I choose to* or *I could.* Try these new words on for size. See if they take the pressure off you.

Put a big sign in your kitchen.
Today I will NOT should on myself.

Read it every morning.

9. SMELL IT AND SMILE

Our sense of smell resides in the limbic region
of our brain, which is the most primal and ancient part.
For over 6000 years we have been stimulating our sense
of smell with fragrant oils, spices, and incense in order
to enhance and alter our moods.

The term aromatherapie was first used in 1928 to
describe the therapeutic effects of aromatic plant essences.
Today Aromatherapy is a means to control mood.
It is used everywhere from boardrooms to football
locker rooms, to health spas to help people feel good.

You can use aromas in your home, office, and
even in the car to soothe, stimulate, and refresh yourself.

Learn what smells make you feel good.
Find the smell that puts a smile on your face.
Common smile smells include cinnamon, freshly baked
bread, cotton candy, oranges, baby powder, and vanilla.

1 0. BE MORE MINDFUL

We live in a hurry-up-gotta-get-it-done world.
Our minds are often scattered and in conflict as we try to do two, three, or even more things at one time. This common habit plays havoc with our mental health.

Focusing our attention and being mindful of just one thing at a time is useful. It is a way to calm ourselves and produce the *relaxation response.*

You can take your mind off one thing by concentrating intently on another. Try this:

Take three entire minutes to eat a raisin.
You can also try this with an unusual flavored jellybean.
Chew slowly and savor each part of the experience.
Be totally present in the moment. Focus on the activity of chewing, savoring, and tasting.

Feel different? Practice this habit of mindfulness everyday, with eating, walking, gardening or even washing dishes.

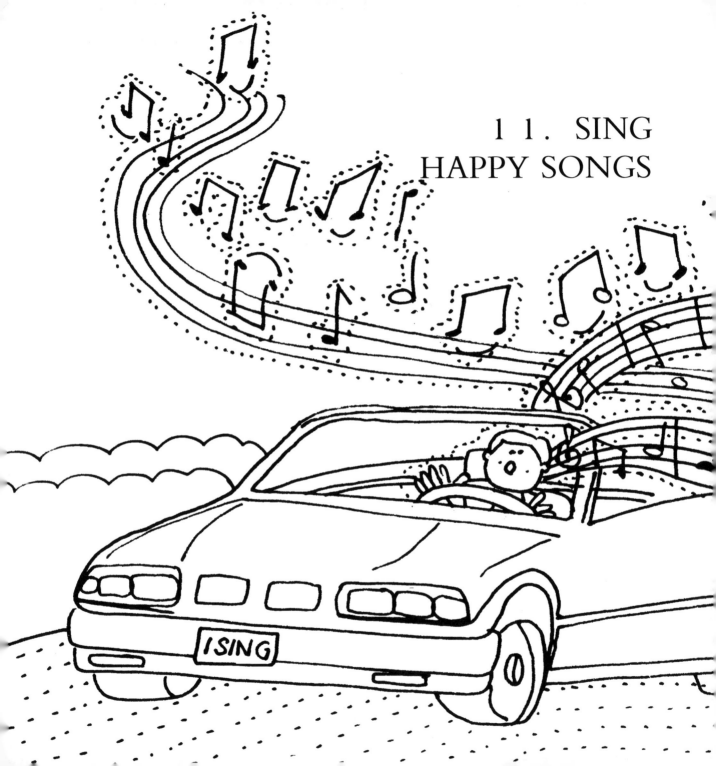

Make an audiotape of happy songs. These can be songs that bring back memories of happy times. Include songs with upbeat tunes and those you want to sing along with. Then sing along. Who cares if you can't sing?

"Jeremiah was a bullfrog. Such a good friend of mine." I go for a car ride and really belt out these tunes. When I get back I feel great. Keep a copy of your tape in the house and the car. Music works wonders.

12. TELL JOKES

Ask a buddy to tell you a joke.

Everyone knows someone who knows a joke.

Call them. Then laugh a lot together.

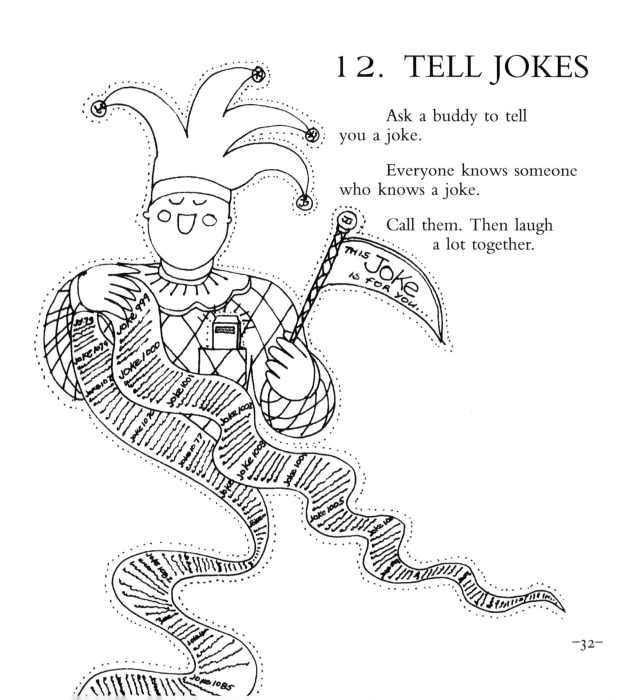

"Laughter is the shortest distance between two people." –Victor Borge

Here's a joke for today:

 Sherlock Holmes and Dr. Watson went on a camping trip. As they lay down for the night, Holmes said: "Watson, look up into the sky and tell me what you see"

Watson said "I see millions and millions of stars".

Holmes: "And what does that tell you?"

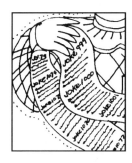 Watson: "Astronomically, it tells me that there are millions of galaxies and potentially billions of planets. Theologically, it tells me that God is great and that we are small and insignificant. Meteorologically, it tells me that we will have a beautiful day tomorrow. What does it tell you?"

Holmes: "Somebody stole our tent".

If you want to find more jokes on the internet, here's what you do:

Go to your favorite search engine (mine is www.google.com) and type in the word "jokes." It will direct you to several "joke" sites that will leave you laughing.

13. READ FUNNY CARDS

Go to the largest card store you can and find and read funny cards until you are smiling, giggling, or laughing.

Warning. Stay out of the mushy *I-miss-you-and-I'll-never-get-over-you-leaving-me* section.

It could be dangerous to your mental health.

14. TAKE A SHORT VACATION

Take a moment to visualize and to explore...
and go on a mini-vacation in your mind.

Where would you really love
to be right now? Does a tropical beach mean
paradise or is your Garden of
Eden in the forest? Or, would you prefer a
cosmopolitan utopia?

Whatever you choose, sit back,
or lie down. Close your eyes, breathe deeply, and
let yourself go there.

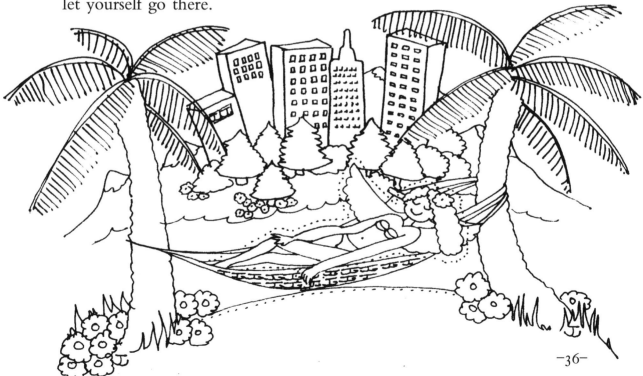

TAKE A 5 MINUTE VACATION

What does your mini vacation look like?
Feel like?
Describe it here:

Your mind doesn't know the difference between something that has actually happened and something vividly imagined.

How wonderful!

_____

_____

_____

_____

_____

_____

_____

_____

_____

_____

_____

15. START A TREASURE ALBUM

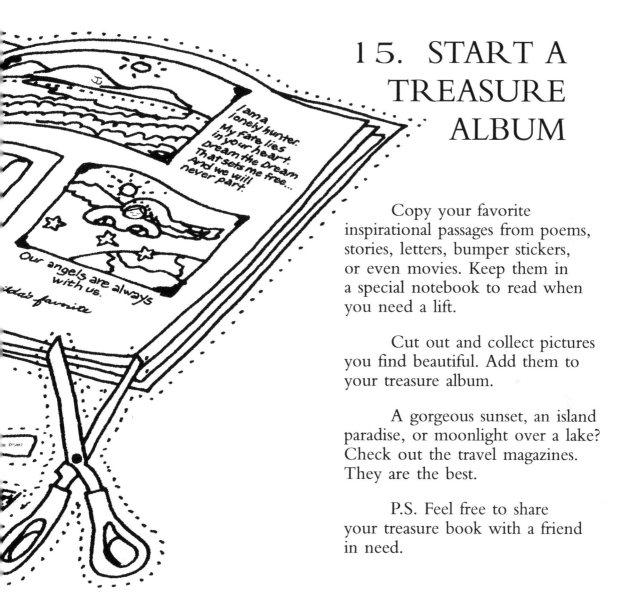

Copy your favorite inspirational passages from poems, stories, letters, bumper stickers, or even movies. Keep them in a special notebook to read when you need a lift.

Cut out and collect pictures you find beautiful. Add them to your treasure album.

A gorgeous sunset, an island paradise, or moonlight over a lake? Check out the travel magazines. They are the best.

P.S. Feel free to share your treasure book with a friend in need.

16. LAUGH

Buy some happy videos. Norman Cousins, who wrote *Anatomy of an Illness*, laughed himself out of a serious illness. Laughter is a great healer and tension-reducer.

Laughter releases happy chemicals, called endorphins, into your brain. Buy a few videos that you know will make you laugh.

An old John Belushi video, *My Cousin Vinnie*, and *Gilda Radnor Live* are in my collection.

17. START YOUR OWN "**14,000** THINGS THAT MAKE ME HAPPY" BOOK

Yes, someone actually wrote a book like that.
Why don't you?

Christmas present in August •352• Taking an early morning stroll while the grass beneath my feet is still moist and wet •353• Celebrating the New Year with my family •354• Buying shirt that makes me feel pretty •355• Going for a drive, with the windows rolled down, jus the fun of it •356• The way I feel right after I get a hair cut •357• Having an acupuncture •358• Taking a long and luxurious bubble bath •359• Organizing my dresser drawers •36 Completing a project for my work, and knowing that I have done a really good job •361• the acknowledgement from a peer who I really respect •362• Birthing, creating and man this book •363• Buying myself a single rose •364• Receiving a single flower from my belo •365• Winning a set at match point •366• Being there for a friend •367• Eating Sushi •368 a bird land on my balcony railing •369• Doing meditation when I wake up in the morning Giving seminars •370• Eating chocolate chip cookies that have just come out of the over Receiving a surprise post card from a friend who I didn't know was on vacation •372• Sp long distance - without watching the clock - for an hour to my friends in Canada •373• Li to gentle jazz •374• Country Dancing •375• Watching the gentle flow and interaction of tr fish and coral in a fish tank •376• Going to a weekend workshop that helps me to better stand, and like myself •377• Teaching •378• Hand drawing a thank you note •379• Ackn a teacher •380• Being grateful that I can think of so many ways to be happy •381• Laying back in the wet morning grass and watching the clouds drifting by •382• Playing with my old niece •383• Watching my Maine Coon kittens romp •384• Playing miniature golf •38! and Illustrating my own New Years cards •386• Calling home to connect with my family • Repotting a plant that has been with me for over 10 years •388• Writing a letter •389• Ap when my taxes are done and I know I'm getting a big refund •390• Going for a sail in the morning •391• Flying up to New York to visit my old friends •392• Reading my favorite po •393• Getting my car washed and shined •394• When I get a good Driver License photo Looking through photographs from my trip to Paris •396• Doing a spontaneous drawing magic markers •397• Hearing carolers sing during the Holiday season •398• Watching m play with her dog •399• Taking out the silver for the holidays •400• Eating matzo ball sou Reading the New York Times Magazine Section •402• When my investments go up •403 a barbecue •404• Renting a video that has a romantic and happy ending •405• Playing g music •406• Having a sip of champagne •407• Swimming •408• Puttering in the garden Sleeping late on a Sunday morning •410• Feeding bread to the ducks •411• Wearing my earrings •412• Opening up Birthday presents •413• Setting a formal dinner table with g

thank you, **THANK YOU**, *thank you*, t h a n k y o u, thank you

thank **you**, *thank you*, thank you, **thank you**, thank you

THANK YOU, *thank you*, thank you, ***thank you***, thank you

thank you, *thank you*, **thank you**, **thank you**, **THANK YOU**

THANK YOU, *thank you*, **thank you**, *thank you*, **thank you**

thank you, **THANK YOU**, thank you, thank you, *thank you*,

THANK YOU, *thank you*, thank you, *thank you*, *thank you*,

thank you, THANK YOU, **thank you**, *thank you*, **THANK YOU**

Thank You, *thank you*, _44_ Thank You, THANK YOU

18. Say *thank you* often. Say *thank you* for your health, your strong body, your intelligence, for your sense of humor, and for your friends.

Just say "thank you." You don't even have to direct it to anyone. Just saying *thank you* often works to expand your capacity for goodness.

the gratitude habit

19. HELP SOMEONE ELSE

No matter how negative you are feeling, chances are there is someone, somewhere, feeling worse than you.

You can move from the negative place you are in by helping someone move from the place they are in.

Cheer up a child. Help out in a soup kitchen. Lend a helping hand in a hospital or around the neighborhood.

Get involved and soon you will begin to appreciate all that you do have.

20. TAKE A NATURE BREAK

Connect with nature.
Take a walk, touch a tree, hold a flower,
feel the clouds. Rediscover how perfect
the world is.

Lie down on the ground
if you can. Imagine you have roots that
run deep into the earth.

Feel the healing energy coming
into your spine.

21. HUG A TREE

My daughter took me into the woods one day and suggested that I hug a tree.

I said I would feel ridiculous doing that. She said, That's okay. Do it anyway. And so I did. It felt wonderful.

In many indigenous cultures, trees are considered the medicine people of the plant kingdom. Throughout the world, many people recognize the connection between nature and healing. Trees symbolize transformation because they change each season.

Even if it does seem a bit silly, try hugging a tree. While you are hugging the tree, put your ear up against the trunk and listen. Perhaps you'll hear its ancient wisdom.

Okay. Okay. I understand this can be hard to do. So try this: Lean up against a tree. Rest your back against its strong trunk. Close your eyes and imagine that the tree is hugging you.

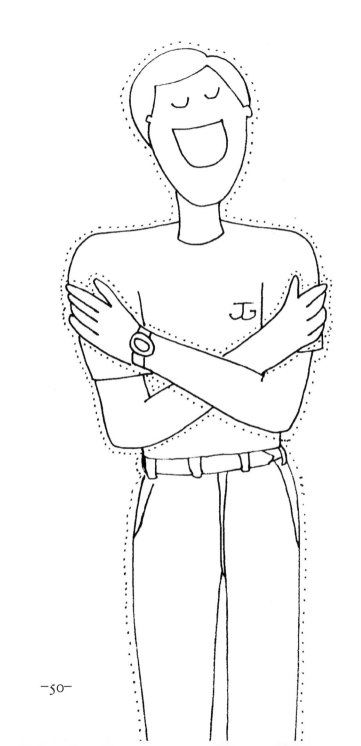

22. HUG YOURSELF

Hug yourself if you can't find anyone to give you a hug.

Wrap your right arm around the left side of your body, and your left arm around the right side of your body. Then giggle about how silly you look while you enjoy the hug.

If you can't bear to be silly, then feel justified knowing you are stretching your trapezius muscles and alleviating back strain.

23. SORT OUT YOUR WORRIES

We all have worries. Sometimes it helps to get them organized and sorted out.

Here is how to do it. Write a worry list. Use as much paper as you need. For three non-stop minutes, list everything that worries you – everything. Then go through your list and sort the things that you <u>can</u> do something about and those you can't do anything about. Transfer them to separate lists.

Take the *Things I can't do anything about* list and rip it into little pieces. Burn it ceremoniously. As you watch the smoke rise and drift away, tell yourself that you are letting go of those things you can't control.

Now go back to the *Things I can do something about* list. Next to each item, write a plan to alleviate that worry. Then put the plan in place.

Believe me, you will feel great.

P.S. We have designed some great forms on the following pages to help you organize your worries. Prepare lots of copies. You will love how relieved you'll feel each time you do this exercise.

Worries 🙂
Things I can do something about

1. Complete all my unfinished projects before my next business trip.

2. Get new health insurance.

3. Call for vacation brochures.

4. Check out tooth ache.

5. Figure out my taxes.

Worries ☹
thing...

1. stop d...
change m...s attitud...
...req...pre...
...thesis ...fferently
...someth'...
4. Unde... conver...
...beg...age
about
help my frien... marriage

Things I Worry About

_____

_____

_____

_____

_____

_____

_____

_____

_____

_____

_____

_____

_____

_____

_____

_____

_____

_____

Things
I Can't Do
Anything
About

Things
I Can Do
Something
About

Here's What
I Intend To Do
Something
About

24. PICK A PRAYER

Copy a passage, poem, or prayer that has special meaning for you. Laminate it and keep it in your wallet.

Read the passage often during difficult times.

I carry a poem from the martial arts with me. A friend carries the *serenity prayer*.

The latest books say prayer, which can also be poems, stories, or fables, works in healing. Prayer even works on others when they are at a distance. Give it a try. It couldn't hurt.

serenity
e things
change,
ge to change
s we can and
dom to know
fference.

DRIVERS
LICENSE

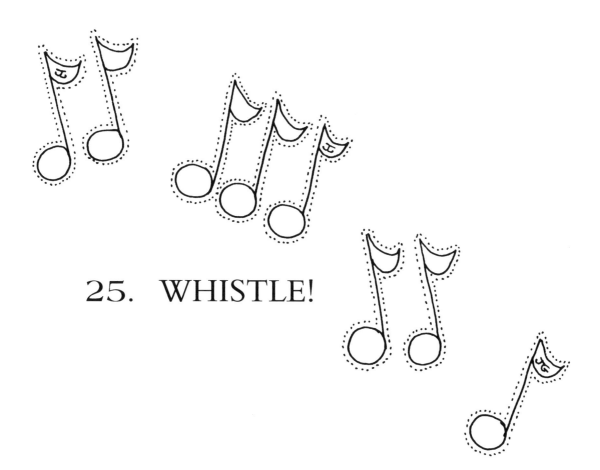

25. WHISTLE!

26. BLOW IT AWAY

Always, always, always keep a jar of bubbles under the sink.

When things get crazy, go outside and blow bubbles. Imagine you are blowing your troubles into the bubbles. Then watch them float away.

When your *trouble-bubbles* are all gone, blow your wishes into new bubbles. Then send your wish bubbles into the world to be fulfilled.

Einstein said imagination is more important than knowledge. Everyone has imagination. Use yours for your wish bubbles.

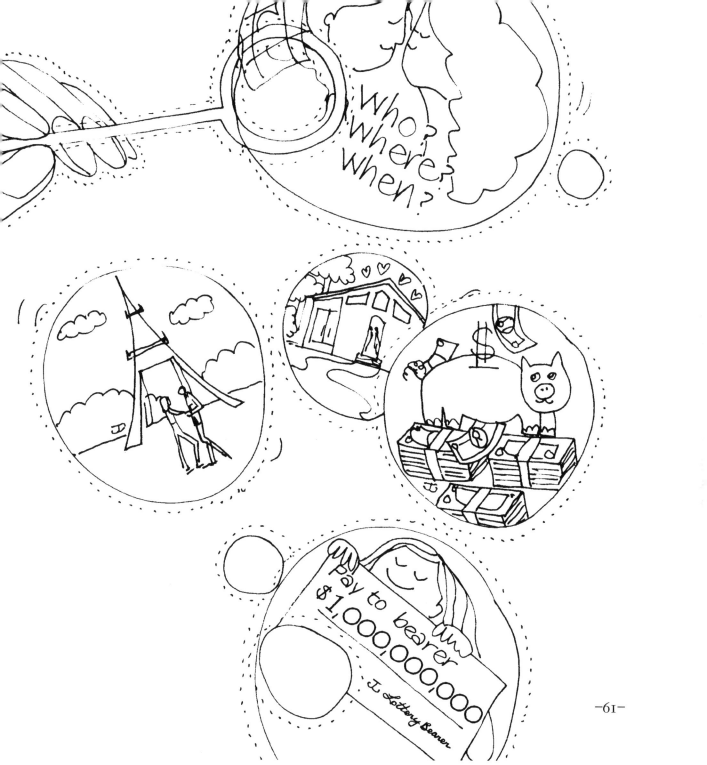

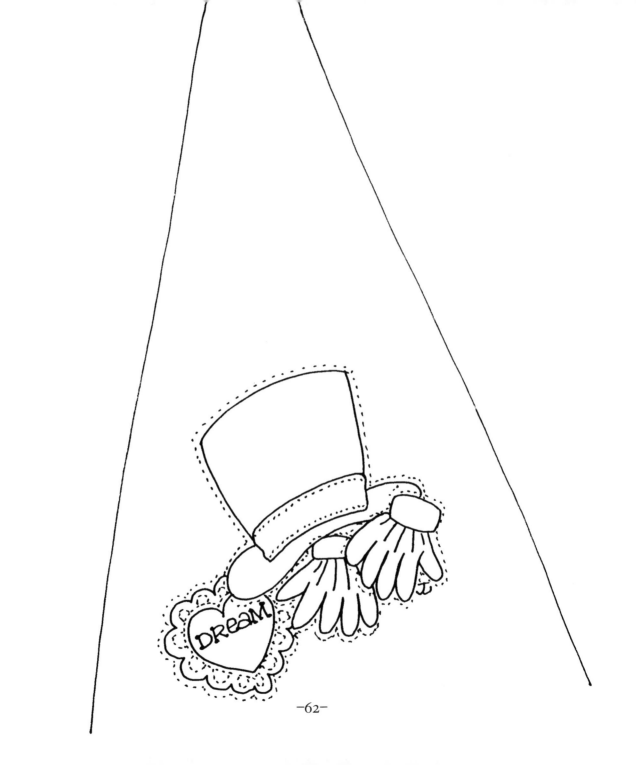

27. BY JIMINY

Many of us don't get what we want because we don't ask for it. Maybe we don't know what's available or what's possible. Maybe we don't know how to ask. Maybe we don't know what we really want or need.

Sit down. Breathe deeply. Take a moment to go into your heart. Ask your heart what it is you really need or want. Then remember what Jiminy Cricket said. *When your heart is in your dream, no request is too extreme.*

Ask for what you want.

28. INDULGE

Pick a splurge. Make it a small but very significant splurge. Indulge yourself and allow that splurge to help you feel better.

We all need to play an active role in changing our state of mind when things get tough. A small indulgence reminds us that we are special. It facilitates a shift in feelings at the same time.

A bubble bath, a glass of champagne, a walk, a hike, a swim, a good novel, a new fishing magazine, an hour off from responsibility.

What are the special treats you might use to shift your mood from blue to bright?

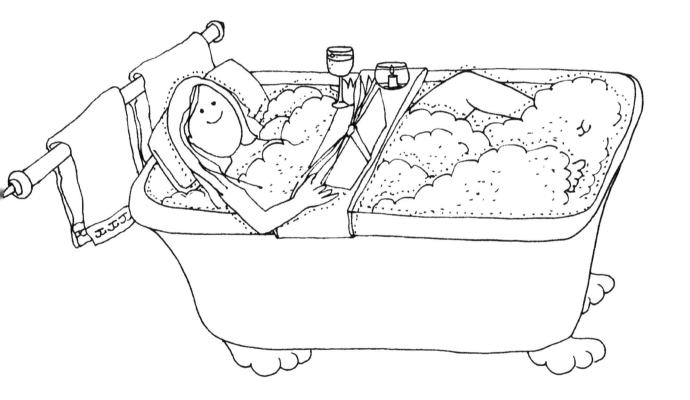

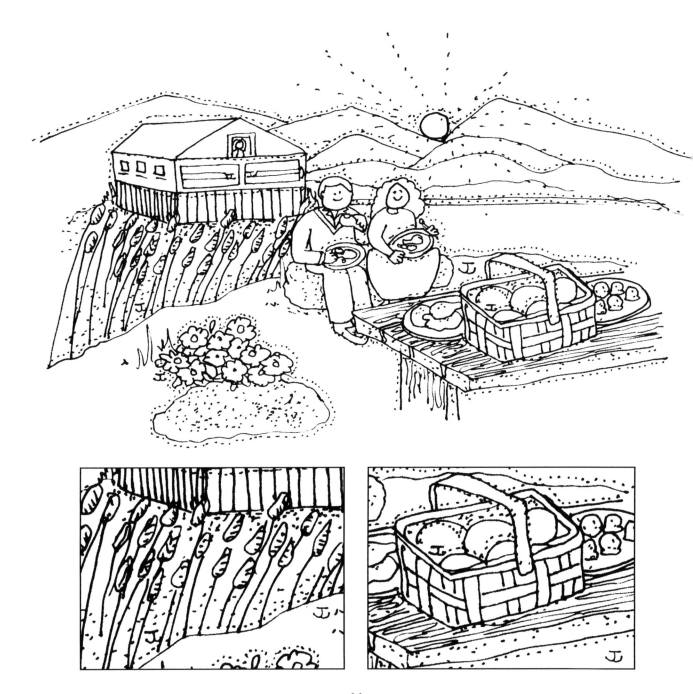

29. THE ART AND GAME OF REFRAME

A single situation can be looked at in dozens of different ways. It all depends on how you *frame* it.

With one kind of frame a picture has a certain look. Crop the image and something new comes into focus. Enlarge it, make it smaller, or cut off the left corner. The result is a different view and perspective of the same picture.

We all form pictures of situations and then respond to our interpretations. By altering the picture we can alter our feelings and our response to the situation. Alter your feelings and you can alter your behavior.

There is a lot of fun to reframing. If you don't like the picture in its new frame, just take it out and put the old one back. No risk.

Play the reframe game. You just might like the view from a different angle.

30. LOOK AT THINGS FROM A NEW PERSPECTIVE

Early in life we develop a preference for either right-handedness or left-handedness. Our right hand and the muscles on the right side of our body are controlled by the left side of our brain. Our left hand and the muscles on the left side are controlled by the right side of the brain.

Through the years we reinforce the use of one side or the other. We form habitual ways of doing things and pattern our brain.

This dependence on one side of our brain can limit access to the other side. Wouldn't you like to know what the other side of your brain is thinking?

To get new perspective on the situation, do the exercise on the next page. It is designed to free you from your habitual ways and open up new pathways in your brain.

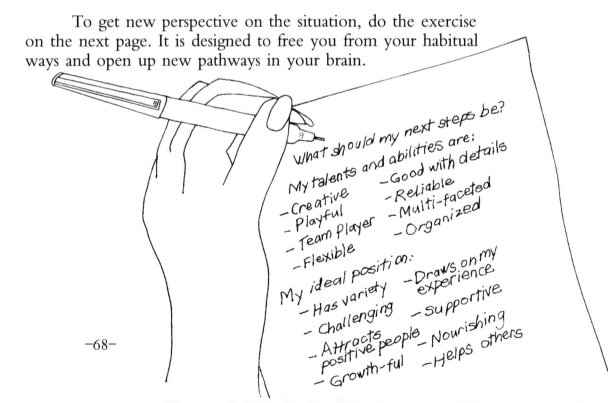

What should my next steps be?

My talents and abilities are:
- Creative
- Playful
- Team player
- Flexible
- Good with details
- Reliable
- Multi-faceted
- Organized

My ideal position:
- Has variety
- Challenging
- Attracts positive people
- Growth-ful
- Draws on my experience
- Supportive
- Nourishing
- Helps others

Do it now!

Sit quietly and calmly for 15 minutes. Be sure to get away from all distractions. Background music is good if you like it. Try something you don't usually listen to.

With the hand you use the most (your dominant hand) take hold of your other hand, which is the non-dominant one. For most people the dominant hand is the right and the non-dominant hand is the left. Begin to massage the non-dominant hand. Gently tug on your fingers. Twist them a bit, rocking each finger from side to side in its socket. Look at your fingers as you do this. Use a sawing motion and saw the spaces in between your fingers. Use the finger of your dominant hand as the saw. Encircle your non-dominant hand at the wrist joint and wiggle your fingers. Enjoy watching your hand dance. Gently loosen up the elbow and shoulder joints on your non-dominant side. This will give you maximum results.

When your non-dominant side is really loose, place a pen in that hand. Ask yourself a question for which you need a new answer. Then begin to write. I bet you will discover many new answers. And you will gain several surprising perspectives.

My question:

_____

_____

_____

New perspectives:

_____

_____

_____

_____

_____

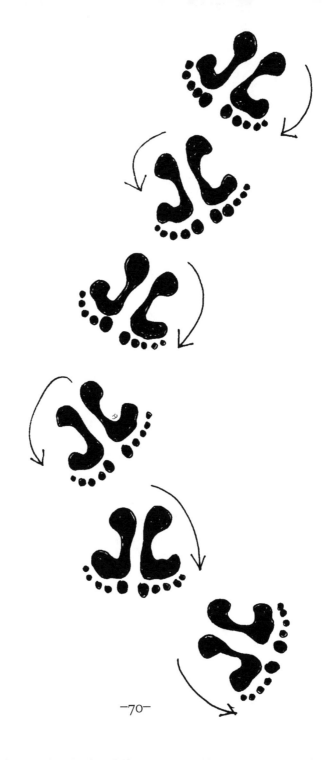

31 . HAPPY FEET

My friend, the redhead, used to cheer me by doing a dance he called *happy feet*. It's a very quick dance done mostly with the feet. He just got his feet bouncing up and down by taking tiny fast steps. At the same time he maintained a look of surprise on his face as if his feet were dancing without permission.

Never once did I fail to smile.

I offer two options: Teach some friends to do *happy feet* and then get their help when you sorely need a giggle. Or, you can do *happy feet* yourself. Just imagine that your two feet have a mind of their own. At any time they can just pop up and start dancing. Enjoy the look of wonder and delight that will break out all over your face.

Now that you know how to do *happy feet*, go out and cheer up a friend.

32. MAKE A NEW STORY OF IT

Everyone has a sad story, or two. It might be the story of the job you lost, the pain you experienced, your disappointments, or the loneliness you feel. Can you turn your story into a movie?
A one-act play?
A stand-up comedy routine?
Can you make the plot funny? Can you turn it into an adventure story?

Maybe you can even turn your story into a cartoon. Scott Adams did with Dilbert®.

Can you create advertisements for your movie? Can you give it different endings?

Of course you can. And after you play with your story for a while, your feelings about it just might change.

33. EXPECT MIRACLES

Miracles do happen. But they happen mostly to those who believe in them.

Miracles come in all shapes and sizes. And they come frequently, once you open the door and invite them in. We all have the power to create miracles in our lives.

When you expect miracles you will find them. And better yet, they will find you.

34. BOOKS! BOOKS! BOOKS!

Dedicate a bookshelf to you. Collect wonderful books. Treat yourself to some beautifully bound and covered favorites.

Anne Morrow Lindberg's *A Gift from the Sea* and Richard Bode's *First You Have to Row a Little Boat* are my favorites.

And how about some picture books with flowers, porcelain, or wooden boats? These are the kinds of books that you can find on a sale table and treasure forever. A bonus is that they are often marked way down in price.

Indulge.

35. MOVE THE FURNITURE

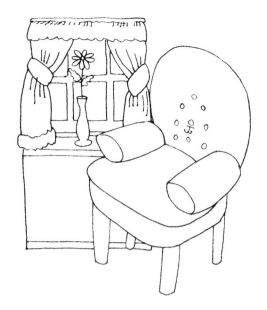

When I'm really stuck in a rut, moving the furniture works wonders to move me out of it. Moving a couch, a desk, or the bed gives me a different viewpoint. It helps me see things from a different angle. Rearranging the pictures on the walls and buying new curtains helps, too.

When my daughter needs a new perspective, she paints the furniture bright colors and decorates it with sunflowers, squiggly lines, or grapevines. She paints all her flowerpots different colors and moves them to new spots. How refreshing!

Change your surroundings often. It keeps you fluid.

36. PRACTICE A RANDOM ACT OF KINDNESS

The world is a little short of kindness. It feels really good to do something to change that.

Give the person at the drive-thru window a flower the next time you are there. Pay the toll for the car behind you. Give your server a 30% tip for lunch and leave a nice note. Bring a bunch of daisies to the clerk at the Motor Vehicle Department. Take a garbage bag and clean up the beach or the park the next time you walk there. Smile at everyone that comes within three feet of you.

The possibilities are endless and so much fun! If you need directions for performing random acts of kindness, there are several books on it.

37. DIAL A-WALLOW

Okay. Sometimes it seems impossible to get out of a bad mood. Make a deal with a close friend to listen and give you a few minutes of wallowing.

I call it Dial-a-Wallow.

Sometimes you just need to get the stuff off your chest.

Here is how it works: You get an allotted amount of uninterrupted time to vent. Your friend provides support with no criticism or advice.

After your time is up, take five very deep breaths together. You can even do this over the phone. Then say thank you.

Of course your friend gets a turn another time.

38. PUT A COACH ON YOUR HEAD AND TAKE A HIKE.

Strap on your walking cassette player and snap in your favorite motivational, educational, or inspirational speaker. Then take an invigorating hike or leisurely stroll.

Whenever you try to modify the *software* in your brain, your ears can serve as a direct path.

When you want to learn something new, you need to listen to it over and over. *My life is joyous and positive. My life is joyous and positive.*

Some of my favorite tapes are:

Wayne Dyer's *Real Magic*, Dan Millman's *Laws of Spirit* and Marianne Williamson's *Enchanted Love*. I love almost anything by Deepak Chopra, Bernie Siegel, Angeles Arrien, Carolyn Myss, and Jack Canfield.

For very little money, you can have expert advice whenever, wherever, and as often as you like.

39. GET HUGGED

Find someone to give you a hug.

Virginia Satir said we need four hugs a day for survival, eight hugs a day for maintenance, and twelve hugs a day for growth.

Most of us have some catching up to do.

40. CLEAN OUT A CLOSET

Get rid of stuff you no longer need.

Tell yourself that you are making space for something new and positive and possible in your life.

You are.

41. GIVE YOUR OLD STUFF AWAY

It becomes someone else's new stuff.

42. MAKE A WISH

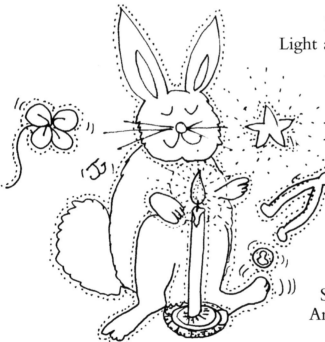

Drop a penny in a fountain. Light a candle and then blow it out.

Wish on a star.

Even in the toughest times, look for hope.

Think about all the generations of people that looked at the stars, the moon, the heavens above, and wished.

Someone wished for you once. And their wish came true.

Here's what I wish:

_____

_____

_____

_____

_____

_____

_____

_____

_____

_____

_____

_____

_____

43. CREATE AN INTENTION

Intention is the spark of Creation. It is the Power behind desire.

When you combine conscious *intention* with focused *attention*, transformation becomes possible.

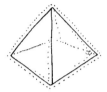

"Where
do sparks fly
for you?"

I intend to:

44. LEARN SOMETHING NEW

Sign up for a course. Learn belly dancing or singing, Japanese cooking, birdhouse construction, or fly-fishing.

A new interest helps take our minds off the every-day stuff.

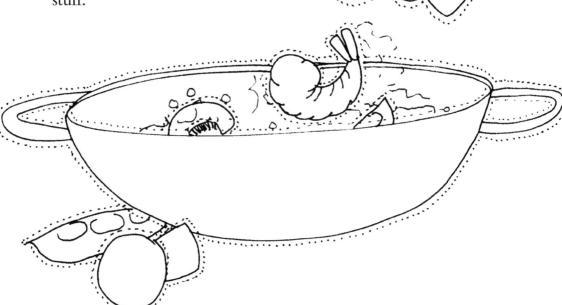

What are some of the
things I always wanted to try?

_____

_____

_____

_____

_____

_____

_____

_____

Which of these
would give me the most joy
if I studied them right now?

_____

_____

Now get up from your chair and grab the yellow pages.
Start with "S" for schools or "E" for education. Find out where
the courses you want are being given, the dates they start,
and how to enroll. Then enroll!

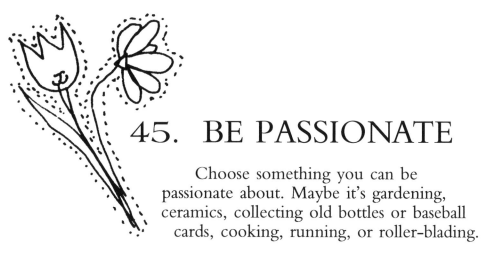

45. BE PASSIONATE

Choose something you can be passionate about. Maybe it's gardening, ceramics, collecting old bottles or baseball cards, cooking, running, or roller-blading.

Then get fully involved in it.
Be there. Be juicy. Be passionate.

46. STIMULATE YOUR ENDORPHINS WITH EXERCISE

Take part in a regular exercise program.

Walk, dance, lift weights, do martial arts, yoga, or kick box. Find something physical you love to do and do it. Regular exercise works the body and prevents depression by releasing endorphins into the blood.

It helps you let go of tension. You benefit from short-term and long-term positive effects.

47. AMUSE YOURSELF

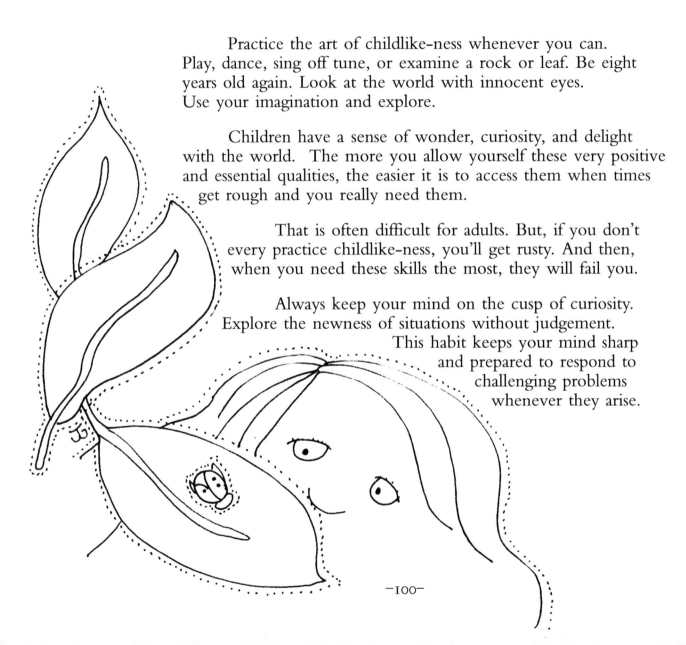

Practice the art of childlike-ness whenever you can.
Play, dance, sing off tune, or examine a rock or leaf. Be eight
years old again. Look at the world with innocent eyes.
Use your imagination and explore.

Children have a sense of wonder, curiosity, and delight
with the world. The more you allow yourself these very positive
and essential qualities, the easier it is to access them when times
get rough and you really need them.

That is often difficult for adults. But, if you don't
every practice childlike-ness, you'll get rusty. And then,
when you need these skills the most, they will fail you.

Always keep your mind on the cusp of curiosity.
Explore the newness of situations without judgement.
This habit keeps your mind sharp
and prepared to respond to
challenging problems
whenever they arise.

"Go ahead. Give yourself permission to be playful. It gets easier the more you do it... and you just might like it!"

– Jo Ann Goldsmith –

"The real voyage of discovery consists not in seeking new landscapes but in having new eyes."

– Marcel Proust–

"To see a world in a grain of sand
And heaven in a wild flower
Hold infinity in the palm of your hand
And eternity in an hour."

– William Blake –

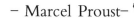

48. REGRESS!

Go to the library or bookstore and head for the children's section. Sit on the floor and read. Or look at the pictures, just like you used to.

Enhance the experience and find a child to read to. Or ask a kid to read to you.

My only coffee table book is Eric Carle's *A House for Hermit Crab.*

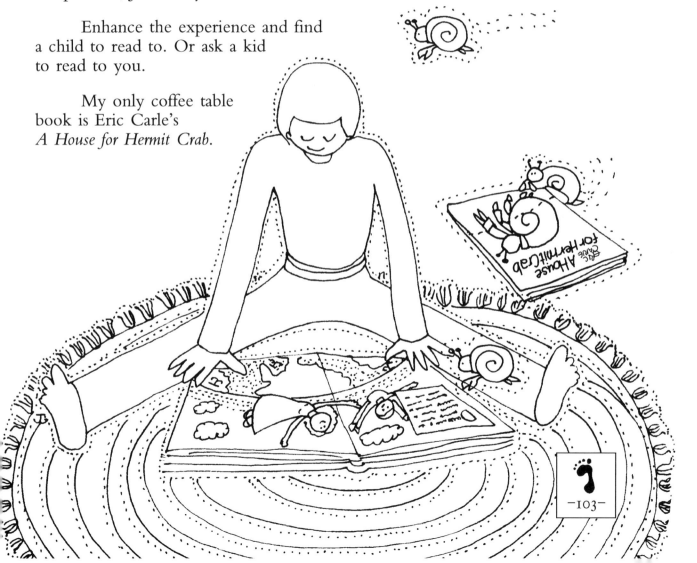

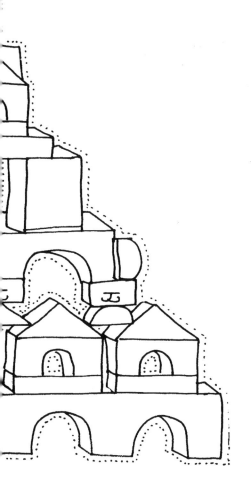

49. TOY TIME

Buy yourself a toy.
March right into a toy store and
buy that favorite toy you lost
when you moved, the one you
could never have, or any one
that suits your fancy.

Let the kids know
that this is your toy.

What does the kid in
you like best?

I'm partial to things
I can build, knock down, and
build up again.

I also love things that
float or fly.

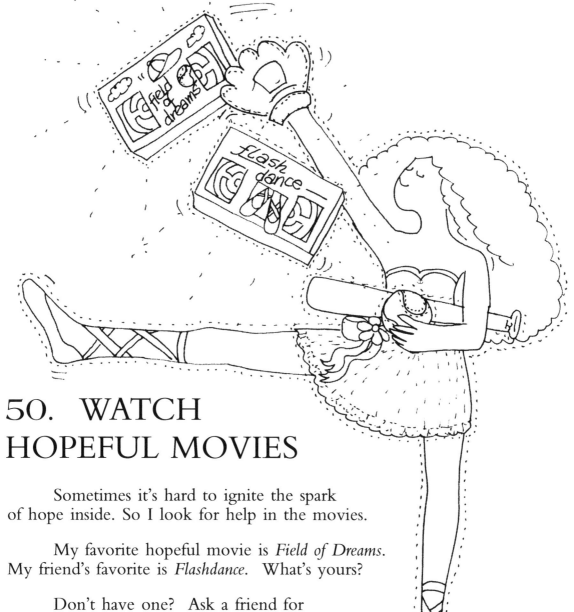

50. WATCH HOPEFUL MOVIES

Sometimes it's hard to ignite the spark of hope inside. So I look for help in the movies.

My favorite hopeful movie is *Field of Dreams*. My friend's favorite is *Flashdance*. What's yours?

Don't have one? Ask a friend for a recommendation or go to the video store and search one out. That part can be the most fun.

Today's Blessings

★ my daughter — how proud I am of her.

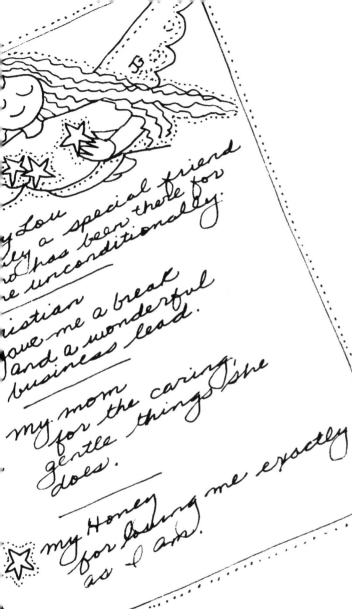

51. BE BLESSED

Buy a beautiful, unlined hardcover book and make it your *Blessings Book*. Write in it often. Write down the names of people and things that are blessings in your life. Include the reasons why.

Refer to your *Blessings Book* often. I keep mine next to my bed. At the end of the day, I write down the blessings, big or small, that came to me that day.

This habit will help you become aware of the many special blessings in your life.

Reading your *Blessings Book* at night puts you in a positive state for peaceful sleep.

52. DONATE MONEY TO THE MAKE-A-WISH FOUNDATION®

Call the Make-A-Wish Foundation,® ask them to tell you about a child who had a wish granted.

Give the foundation a donation and be part of making a sick child happy. Be part of creating magic.

Feel the gesture in your heart. Send some of your warm heart delights to that child. It will make you both feel good.

53. TAKE A "LIVE LIKE A TOURIST" DAY

Once a week, month, or once a quarter take a *"Live Like A Tourist Day"*. Create a list of all the fabulous things your town has to offer like monuments, libraries, museums, or beaches.

Prepare another list of all those attractions you haven't visited. Then take the time to explore your own world; your own backyard. It's great fun when you dress up like a tourist, and eat where the tourists eat. It's a different and delightful experience, and an instant vacation.

What's New
and Nifty
in my backyard.

Nifty places
I want to
explore.

_____
_____
_____
_____
_____
_____
_____
_____
_____
_____
_____
_____

_____
_____
_____
_____
_____
_____
_____
_____
_____
_____
_____

54. CELEBRATE

Most people are good at celebrating birthdays, anniversaries, graduations and weddings. But the art of true celebration lies in the ability to celebrate life itself. Each and every glorious moment of it.

Celebration begins with recognition, the recognition of accomplishment, the recognition of failures and the lessons learned. The recognition that every moment of life has the potential to be celebrate-able. Even the last.

So today, ask yourself, "Did I recognize and celebrate the things that made me proud? Did I recognize and celebrate the beauty of life and the lessons I earned?"

The celebration I speak of is not just that of party hats and fancy cakes. It is the spiritual celebration of all Father/Mother God's creations and yours. We are all creators.

Celebrate Every Day!

FOOTNOTES & ADDITIONAL RESOURCES

1. BREATHE DEEPLY - PAGE 10

Dan Millman, "The Laws of Spirit" – 1995: H J Kramer

Gael Chiarella, "Yokibics® - A Mind-Body Workbook for Everyday Living" – 1992: Yokibics

"Working with breath is a form of spiritual practice. It is also one that impacts health and healing, because how we breathe both reflects the state of the nervous system and influences the state of the nervous system". Andrew Weil, M.D. "Spontaneous Healing" – 1995 Ballantine Books

2. VISUALIZE - PAGE 13

"Creative visualization is the technique of using your imagination to create what you want in your life, create a clear image of something you wish to manifest. Then you continue to focus on the idea or picture regularly, giving it positive energy until it becomes objective reality". Shakti Gawain, "Creative Visualization" – 1978: Bantam Books

The technique of Visualization, the act of imagining or picturing in your mind a more positive state, has been used with athletes to improve performance, with business people to relieve stress and relax, and even with cancer patients to aid in their healing. In the last ten years volumes have been written on the powerful connection between mind and body. Almost any of the works by Dr. Bernie Siegel, Dr. Deepak Chopra, Dr. Joan Borysenko or Dr. Andrew Weil will be helpful in mastering the art of visualization. The mind body connection is explored in the fields now known as Psychoneuroimmunology and Neuro-Linguistics.

5. PROGRAM YOUR MIND - PAGE 19

The mind communicates with the body through language, thought, image and metaphor, and the body responds. To learn more about this powerful connection study the teachers mentioned in the Visualization section and read "Your Body Believes Every Word You Say" by Barbara Hoberman Levine, 1991, Aslan Publishing

"Affirming by statement is a natural method of manifestation that we have been unconsciously using all along. Each of the 50,000 thoughts we have each day is actually an affirmation - positive or negative - and each is bringing about change in our lives, accordingly. We need to be aware of what we are programming! We want to assertively program positive thoughts so that we reap positive results". Ruth Ross, Ph.D., "Prospering Woman" – 1982: New World World Library

9. SMELL IT AND SMILE - PAGE 27

The benefits of inhaling sweet aromas, indulging in expensive perfumes, taking in the scent of a bouquet of fresh flowers, or filling the house with fragrant potpourris seem obvious, yet the healing powers of scent are various and complex in the ancient art of aromatherapy, in which distilled essential oils of certain plants are used for specific benefits in therapy and natural health. To understand more about aromatherapy, I recommend "The Essential Aromatherapy," it explores the wonderful powers and benefits of herbs, essential oils, and scents as well as the practice of one of the world's most ancient natural therapies.

Carole McGilvery and Jim Reed, "The Essential Aromatherapy: A Comprehensive Guide to Using Essential Oils for Health, Relaxation and Pleasure," Anness Publishing Limited – 1994; London England – 1999: Hermes House

10. BE MORE MINDFUL - PAGE 29

Jon Kabat-Zinn of the University of Massachusetts Medical Center in Worcester MA has a well researched clinical program that promotes the benefits of the practice of mindfulness meditation. He found that this ancient practice of moment to moment awareness can help alleviate chronic pain and reduce stress. Kabat-Zinn focuses on "mindfulness,"

FOOTNOTES & ADDITIONAL RESOURCES

a concept that involves living in the moment, paying attention, and simply "being" rather than "doing."

While you can practice anything "mindfully," from taking a walk to cleaning your house, Kabat-Zinn presents several meditation techniques that focus the attention most clearly, whether it's on a simple phrase, your breathing, or various parts of your body.

Jon Kabat-Zinn:

> "Wherever You Go There You Are: Mindfulness Meditation in Everyday Life" – 1995: Hyperion

> "Mindfulness Meditation: Cultivating the Wisdom of Your Body & Mind" – 1995: Simon & Schuster (Audio)

> "Full Catastrophe Living: Using the Wisdom of Your Body & Mind to Face Stress, Pain and Illness" Reprint edition – 1990: Delta

Dr. Herbert Benson pioneered the original thinking on the idea of the "relaxation response." When we elicit the response through breathing, or gentle repetition of words there are physiological changes in our body. Our metabolism, blood pressure, heart rate, and blood flow to our extremities all decrease. These changes are exactly the opposite of the physiological changes that occur during the fight or flight response, which is typically evoked during stress.

Herbert Benson, "The Relaxation Response" – 1975: William Morrow

11. SING HAPPY SONGS - PAGE 31

Three Dog Night, "Joy to the World" – The Big Chill – Original Motion Picture SoundTrack

1983: Motown Record Company

1 6. LAUGH – PAGE 41

Norman Cousins "Anatomy of an Illness as Perceived by the Patient" – 1991: Bantam Doubleday Dell

"My Cousin Vinnie" VHS – 1992
(Not for sale to persons under age 18.) Twentieth Century Fox

"Gilda Radnor Live" VHS – 1980: Time Warner
(Not for sale to persons under age 18.)

1 7. START YOUR OWN "14,000 THINGS THAT MAKE ME HAPPY" BOOK – PAGE 42

Barbara Ann Kipfer kept notebooks all her life. In those notebooks she collected all of the little things that made her happy. She used her collection to cheer herself up, get ideas about what to cook for dinner or something fun to do. Barbara believes that happiness comes from noticing and enjoying the little things in life.

Barbara Ann Kipfer "14,000 Things to be Happy About" – 1990: Workman Publishing

24. PICK A PRAYER – PAGE 56

Interesting new evidence abounds that prayer works in healing. Double blind scientific studies carried out by reputable institutions are "proving" that prayer has a part in healing.

Larry Dossey, "The Healing Power of Prayer" – 1998: Harpercollins

Larry Dossey, (Editor) John Kabat-Zinn, Sogyal Rinpoche, Jack Kornfield and Michael Toms, "The Power of Meditation and Prayer" – 1997: Hay House

27. BY JIMINY - PAGE 63

Jiminy Crickett is a character invented by Walt Disney. His quote, "When your heart is in your dream, no request is too extreme," comes from Walt Disney's Pinocchio – 1940

If you want to learn more about how to ask for the things you want, read:

Jack Canfield and Mark Victor Hansen, "The Aladdin Factor" – 1995: Berkley Pub Group

32. MAKE A NEW STORY OF IT – PAGE 73

"Dilbert" is a registered trademark of United Feature Syndicate, Inc.

Dilbert®, the cartoon hero of the office cubicle, is a character created by Scott Adams in 1989. Today the cartoon appears in more than 2,000 newspapers in 56 countries. There are 22 Dilbert Books with over 10 million copies in print. Dibert.com was the first syndicated comic strip to go online and is the most widely read syndicated comic on the Internet. One of my favorites is:

Scott Adams, "Dilbert Gives You the Business" – 1999: Andrews McMeel

33. EXPECT MIRACLES – PAGE 75

Stuart Wilde, "Miracles" Reissue Edition – 1995: Hay House

Yitta Halberstam Mandelbaum, Judith Leventhal "Small Miracles : Extraordinary Coincidences from Everyday Life" – 1997: Adams Media Corporation

Bernie S. Siegel, "Love, Medicine and Miracles: Lessons Learned

About Self-Healing from a Surgeon's Experience With Exceptional Patients" – 1990: Harperperennial Library

34. BOOKS, BOOKS, BOOKS – PAGE 77

Richard Bode, "First You Have to Row A Little Boat" – 1993: Warner Books

Anne Morrow Lindbergh, "Gift From the Sea" – 1955, 1975: Random House Inc.

36. PRACTICE A RANDOM ACT OF KINDNESS – PAGE 80

Anne Herbert, "Random Acts of Kindness and Senseless Acts of Beauty" – Margaret M. Pavel (Contributor), Mayumi Oda (Illustrator): Volcano Press

"Random Acts of Kindness" by Conari Press (Editor), Dawna Markova (Introduction), Daphne Rose Kingma – January 1993: Conari Press

Mary K. Colf, Len Oszustowicz, "301 Random Acts of Kindness: A User's Guide to a Giving Life" – June 1994: Summit Pub Group

Meladee McCarty, Hanoch McCarty, "Acts of Kindness: How to Create a Kindness Revolution" – 1994: Health Communications

38. PUT A COACH ON YOUR HEAD AND TAKE A HIKE – PAGE 84

Wayne Dyer, "Real Magic" – 1992: Harper Collins Audio

Deepak Chopra, Wayne W. Dyer, "How to Get What You Really, Really, Really Want" – July 1998: Hay House, Inc.

Dan Millman, "Laws of Spirit" – 1986: Sounds True Catalog

FOOTNOTES & ADDITIONAL RESOURCES

Marianne Williamson, "Enchanted Love" – 1999: Simon & Schuster Audio

Deepak Chopra:

"Ageless Body, Timeless Mind: The Quantum Alternative to Growing Old." Reissue Edition – 1998: Three Rivers Press

"The Seven Spiritual Laws of Success: A Practical Guide to the Fulfillment of Your Dreams" – 1995: Amber-Allen Pub.

"Creating Health: How to Wake Up the Body's Intelligence" – 1995: Houghton Mifflin Co.

Bernie S. Siegel:

"Love, Medicine and Miracles: Lessons Learned About Self-Healing from a Surgeon's Experience With Exceptional Patients" – 1990: Harperperennial Library

"Peace, Love and Healing: Bodymind Communication and the Path to Self-Healing: An Exploration" – 1990: Harperperennial Library

"Personal Reflections and Meditations: A Journey Through Four Guided Meditations for Physical and Spiritual Healing" – 1991: Harper Audio

Angeles Arrien:

"The Four-Fold Way: Walking the Paths of the Warrior, Teacher, Healer, and Visionary" – 1993: Harper San Francisco

"The Second Half of Life" – 1998: Sounds True Catalog

Caroline Myss:

"Anatomy of the Spirit: The Seven Stages of Power and Healing" – 1997: Random House

"Why People Don't Heal and How They Can" – 1998: Three Rivers Press

Jack Canfield:

"Dare to Win" by Jack Canfield, Mark Victor Hansen (Contributor) – 1996: Berkley Publishing Group

"The Aladdin Factor" – 1995: Berkley Pub Group

"How to Build High Self Esteem" – 1989: Nightingale-Conant Corporation

"Chicken Soup for the Soul: 101 Stories to Open the Heart & Rekindle the Spirit" (Chicken Soup for the Soul Series 1-6) Revised edition – 1995: Health Communications

39. GET HUGGED – PAGE 87

Virginia Satir: "Making Contact" – 1976: Celestial Arts

43. CREATE AN INTENTION – PAGE 92

Deepak Chopra, M.D.:

"Attention and Intention: Awareness always has these two components. Attention focuses awareness to a local perception.

FOOTNOTES & ADDITIONAL RESOURCES

Intention brings about a change in that localization."

"Intention is the active partner of attention; it is the way we convert automatic processes into conscious ones."

"Ageless Body, Timeless Mind" – 1993:
Harmony Books, a division of Crown Publishers, Inc.

48. REGRESS! - PAGE 103

Eric Carle "A House for Hermit Crab" – 1987:
Picture Book Studio, Saxonville, MA

50. WATCH HOPEFUL MOVIES – PAGE 107

Kevin Costner, Field of Dreams (VHS) – 1989:
MCA Universal

Jennifer Beal, "Flashdance" (VHS) – 1983: Paramount

52. DONATE MONEY TO THE MAKE-A-WISH FOUNDATION® – PAGE 111

To donate, please call 1-800-722-WISH
or visit the Make-A-Wish Foundation® global website
http://www.wish.org

54 Ways
To Stay Positive
in a Changing, Challenging
And Sometimes NEGATIVE World.

Simple Choices
For More Positive Living

Written By JoAnna Brandi
Illustrated By Jo Ann Goldsmith

TO ORDER
MORE "54 Ways"

When we showed advance copies of this book to our friends and family they all had a similar response, "I love it! Hurry up and get it published, I'd like to buy several copies to send to all my friends!" So just in case you have a similar response here's an easy way to get more copies for your friends, family and co-workers.

1 - 20	Copies	$14.95 each
21 - 50	Copies	$13.95 each
51+	Copies	$12.95 each

MORE BOOKS

If you'd like to learn more about Customer Caring, JoAnna's other books are available as well.

"BUILDING CUSTOMER LOYALTY- 21 ESSENTIAL ELEMENTS IN ACTION"

(Walk the Talk Publishing, 2001)

A handbook focused on building the "emotional attachment" to customers. Easy to read and easy to implement ideas on building better and longer lasting customer relationships. $9.95 each.

"WINNING AT CUSTOMER RETENTION, 101 WAYS TO KEEP 'EM HAPPY, KEEP 'EM LOYAL, AND KEEP 'EM COMING BACK"

(Lakewood Publishing, 1995)

Buy copies for your whole work team and get them all on the same page! A 5% increase in customer retention can double your bottom line profits! $10.95 each.

Volume discounts start at 20 copies. Please call for information. 561-279-0027

FL residents please include 6% sales tax.
Shipping and Handling (Continental US):
SINGLE COPY ORDER $5.95.

MULTIPLE COPY ORDERS
$5.00 plus 7% of total book order.
VISA, MASTERCARD & AMERICAN EXPRESS.

TO ORDER: CALL, WRITE OR FAX to:
JoAnna Brandi & Company
7491 N. Federal Hwy, C-5 #304
Boca Raton, FL 33487
561-279-0027   Fax: 561-279-9400
Email JoAnna Brandi at: joanna@customerretention.com

Find JoAnna on the Web at: www.54simplechoices.com
& at: www.customerretention.com where you can
sign up for JoAnna's FREE TIPS!

Contact Jo Ann at:
Jo Ann Goldsmith
Goldsmithing Enterprises
6216 Barton Creek Circle, Lake Worth, FL 33463
561-963-6426   Fax: 561-432-8207
Email Jo Ann at: joann@creategoldmines.com

Find Jo Ann on the web at: www.creategoldmines.com

***WHEN ORDERING,
PLEASE BE SURE TO INCLUDE:** your name, address, phone number, fax number, email address as well as your credit card number with each order.*

ABOUT JO ANN GOLDSMITH

Jo Ann Goldsmith helps small businesses to *"Create Goldmines."* Her company, *Goldsmithing Enterprises*, specializes in the Art of Corporate Imaging. She creates print & web advertising with the high impact needed in today's competitive arena.

Jo Ann is invaluable to her small business clients, drawing her keen insights and marketing strategies from years of experience with large New York advertising agencies and well known National Clients.

Her joy is in translating the large strategies of a "Procter & Gamble" and a "Hanes Pantyhose" and inspiring and helping smaller businesses to be all they can be. After many years of merging corporate and entrepreneurial experience, Jo Ann creates conceptual graphics and crafts Illustrations that are unique, user friendly and capture the spirit and visions of her clients.

Jo Ann's original illustrations are drawn from her meditations with an "eye towards touching the inner soul" of the person viewing her drawings. Her clients use her original illustrations on their business cards, stationery, brochures, newsletters, greeting cards, advertising, other promotional items and on web sites.

Twenty-five of Jo Ann's illustrations can be enjoyed in Prentice Hall's Book and Training Tape: *"Sweet Persuasion, The Illustrated Art of Closing A Sale"* by Paul Karasik. Additionally, many of Jo Ann Goldsmith's Advertising Illustrations have been published nationally in newspapers and magazine advertisements. She has also done special assignment illustrations for Ottenheimer Publishing.

Ms. Goldsmith is a licensed Minister and a Flow Alignment & Connection™ Practitioner. She has taught meditation and has led workshops in several healing modalities.

Jo Ann loves country dancing and can often be found on a Saturday night doing the "Two-Step" with her husband, Bill. One of her passions is raising Maine Coon Cats – she is often inspired by their agility, playfulness, honesty and ability to simply "be themselves." She's even used this playfulness to "hide" her "JG" logo in most of this book's illustrations. Can You find them?

She studies Tai Chi – The Royal Dragon Form – and integrates its' calming principles into her everyday life and business.

ABOUT JOANNA BRANDI

JoAnna Brandi is a writer, a public speaker and a consultant. She is known in the business world as the 'Customer Care Lady.' She has been in the field of marketing and customer retention and loyalty for over 20 years. A highly rated public speaker in the business sector, her style is uplifting and inspirational as she challenges her audiences to go beyond customer service and start delivering exquisite customer care. Her rallying cry is 'Dare to Care!' SM

She began writing newsletters in 1984 and continues to this day. Her latest, an email tip, reaches thousands of subscribers every other week with inspiration and ideas about caring in the workplace. She is the author of two books, '*Winning at Customer Retention, 101 Ways to Keep 'em Happy, Keep 'em Loyal, and Keep 'em Coming Back*' and '*Building Customer Loyalty-21 Essential Elements in Action.*' She, along with her photographer daughter, Jeanine Brandi, has designed two lines of postcards to help business people 'communicate with caring.' She believes that business needs to be a potent force for positive change in the world and is actively developing programs and products that spread the word. Her library of articles on business can be found at www.customerretention.com.

She is passionate about her own evolution and learning and to that end reads books and attends workshops on spirituality, wellness, and fitness. She dances, does yoga, walks on the beach, journals, and spends time with friends to balance her life. She and illustrator Jo Ann Goldsmith are already busy compiling the next '54 Ways' book, and putting their heads together to develop products that will help their readers stay positive in a changing, challenging, and yes, sometimes even negative world.